70

years of
craftsmanship
to feel

TEXT
Cristina Morozzi

GRAPHIC DESIGN, PAGE LAYOUT AND EDITORIAL COORDINATION
PEPE *nymi*

ART DIRECTOR
Stefano Rossetti

GRAPHIC DESIGNER
Daniela Arnoldo

TRANSLATION
Stefan Chojnicki

First published in the United States of America in 2016 by
Rizzoli International Publications, Inc.
300 Park Avenue South
New York, NY 10010
www.rizzoliusa.com

Originally published in Italian in 2015 by
RCS Libri S.p.A.

2016 2017 2018 2019 / 10 9 8 7 6 5 4 3 2 1

ISBN: 978-0-8478-4908-6

Library of Congress Control Number: 2015945441

Printed in Italy

MORESCHI

THE ITALIAN ART OF SHOEMAKING

WORKS OF ART IN LEATHER

EDITED BY
CRISTINA MOROZZI

RIZZOLI
NEW YORK

New York · Paris · London · Milan

Dedico 70 anni di lavoro della
mia famiglia ai miei collaboratori
con i quali ho condiviso nel
tempo esperienze intense e umane

GianBeppe Moreschi

"I dedicate the seventy years of my family's work to all the people that collaborated
with me, with whom I have shared intense human experiences over the years."

GIANBEPPE MORESCHI

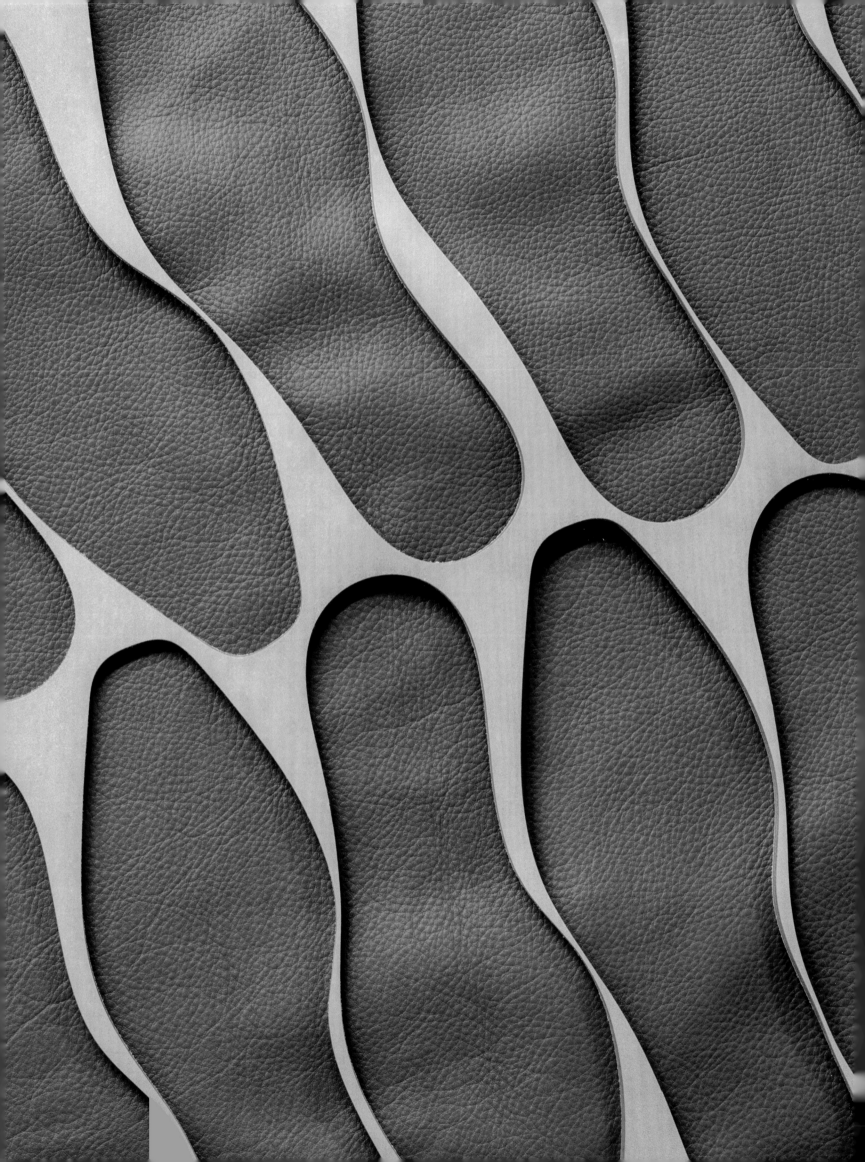

CONTENTS

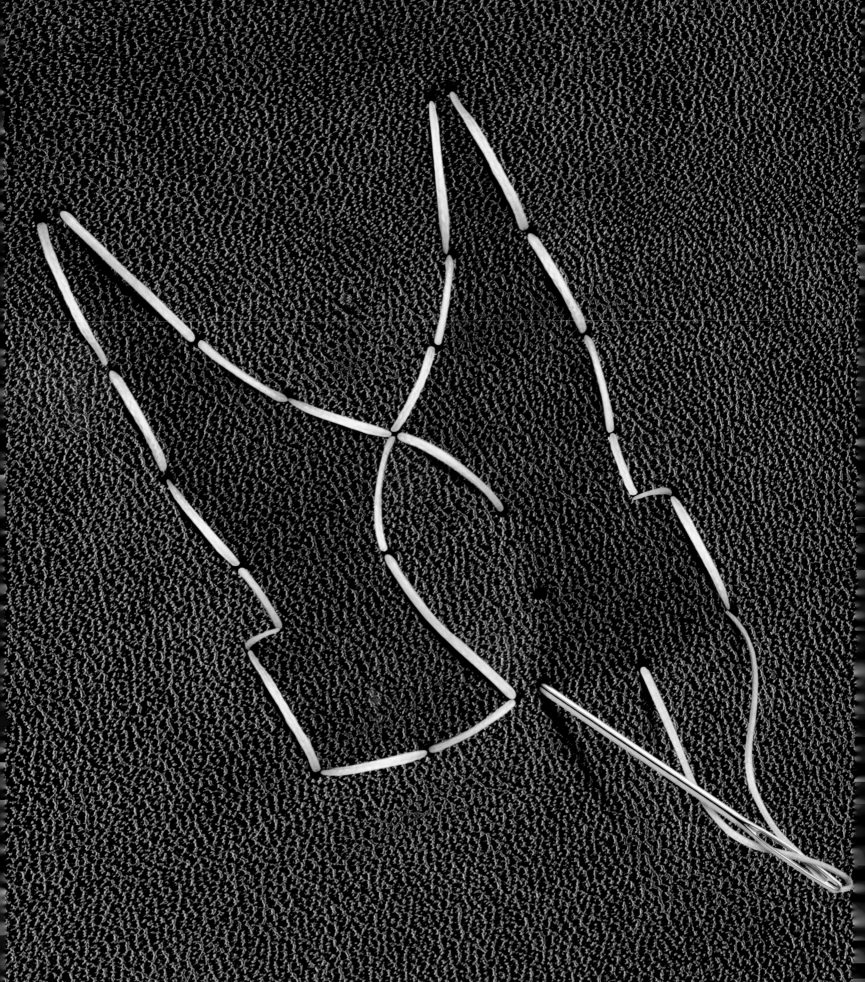

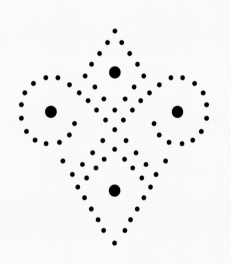

THE M OF
MORESCHI

A PAIR OF STYLIZED
MEN'S SHOES,
BLACK ON WHITE,
FORMING AN M,
DESIGNED BY AG FRONZONI,
IS THE SYMBOL
OF THE SHOEMAKING
WORKSHOP
OF MORESCHI OF VIGEVANO.

The statue of San Giovanni Nepomuceno in Piazza Ducale,
facing the cathedral.

If you head to Vigevano, a town of 63,387 inhabitants in the province of Pavia, from Lorenteggio, Milan, and skirt alongside the natural park of the Ticino Valley before arriving at Piazza Ducale, a large square overlooked by a tower, you will find an industrial area populated primarily with shoe factories. There, flying as a banner, amidst a circular clearing of neatly kept plants planted by Ernesto Pozzi, is a bold white "M" formed from a pair of men's shoes. It is the trademark of Moreschi, the historic Vigevano shoe company, and was designed by Angelo Gabriele Fronzoni in 1963 at the behest of GianBeppe Moreschi who, since 1957, has been the head of the company started by his father Mario in 1946.

Piazza Ducale in Vigevano.

MARIO'S STORY

GianBeppe happily tells the story of his father. His memory is vivid, sketching out people and events with remarkable detail. Gathering both dates and details, he tells the history of the company that belongs to him and his children, and that originally belonged to his father, Mario. He was a man with an unquenchable thirst for life and adventure who died a sudden, untimely death without being able to enjoy the fruit of his work and talent. Having graduated with a qualification for textile work, Mario was a self-taught footwear maker. GianBeppe still keeps his weaving warp notebooks, which, in their meticulous order and detail, look like works of graphic art. He remembers how he delighted in playing the piano and that he used to conduct the Moreschi orchestra. He shows a yellowed image of his father at the controls of a small airplane—he was also a licensed pilot. Stamped on his mind is the image of Armando Capellaro, cousin and electrician, who lived with them and who Mario sent across Italy to sell shoes. "He told him, 'Stop where you see a bell tower because that means there's a town. If you see Magli or Zenith shoe shops or Varese shoemaking, better still, because those are proper shops.'"

"I began shadowing my father when I was twenty," he remembers, "and I learned the job. He was proud of me and used to repeat 'my son's the one keeping me on my feet, he's even sold the chairs.' The factory became too small for me," GianBeppe asserts, "we needed to sell more. I started to travel around Italy by bus with Angelo Carimati visiting clients. I used to be away three or four days a week. Being on the road was all we needed to make sales." He remembers Erminia Zabro, the first shoe finisher, and his sister who worked with him for ten years until she got married.

He has heartfelt words for his schoolmate from the Casale Institute of Accountancy in Vigevano, Giuseppe De Paoli, his best friend and an upright, farsighted man of solid principles. Thanks to the bond of friendship and respect between them, Giuseppe decided to continue working at the Moreschi factory, despite his successful application for work in the railway system. He cut his teeth in the factory, learning the job through hard work and honesty, and became GianBeppe's right-hand man. Giuseppe De Paoli dedicated his life to Moreschi, continuing to work there until December 1999. He passed away prematurely a few months later.

Above, from the left: Mario Moreschi at a ski run at Busancano, in Oropa, Italy, in winter, 1937; GianBeppe Moreschi and Giuseppe De Paoli in 1972.
Below: The airplane that ignited Mario's passion for flying (1934); the grade-one pilot's license and the aircraft license that Moreschi obtained in 1937.

22

Below: National holiday in August 1957 at Montesinaro (Biella), the last holiday with all of the family. Mario Moreschi dies on November 9.

Above: GBM in 1957, the year Mario died and he entered the world of work.
Left: GBM at Coggiola in 1946.

Were it not for the demands of time, GianBeppe could go on speaking for hours in great detail. He depicts people and places as if they belonged in an old film, taking pleasure in the steady development of the business he attends every day in order to carry on the spirit of its adventurous founder, whose choice of clothing revealed an interest in elegant detail even from a young age. He remembers his mother, Iolanda Olivetti, who met Mario Moreschi when she was only nineteen and was immediately won over by this "brilliant young man" who delighted in playing the piano in the bar below her home. GianBeppe loves to celebrate the qualities of his father, whom he holds in the highest esteem. He describes him as self-taught, passionate about culture, and an avid reader across genres. He loves getting out the family album with its yellowed photographs.

He pauses over photos of his father: in shorts playing football, or in a tuxedo conducting the Moreschi orchestra, which he had set up to satisfy his passion for music (he was a very good piano player). He points out Mario dressed as an aviator on board a small 1930s airplane, after obtaining his pilot's license. His passion for flying had remained undiminished from the time he was a young man and had left for Libya as a volunteer. To highlight his father's innate sense of elegance, GianBeppe shows a photo of Mario on honeymoon in 1932 in plus fours trousers with an impeccable dark suit jacket and regimental tie, and another of him, this time in the 1950s, in business attire with a pinstripe suit, Borsalino hat, white handkerchief, and a Montblanc pen inserted in his breast pocket. He remembers his father's entrepreneurialism, his firm commitment to quality production, the successes, and the strains. He remembers him sitting at his desk, head in hands, thinking of work, of commitments undertaken, and of how to pay his employees at the end of the month. The history of Mario and of Morres (the original name of the company) is tied up with that of the Vigevano shoe district; and in the postwar climate of confidence, it thrived. In the photo album, there are pictures of the Morres stand at the Vigevano shoe exhibition, which at the end of the 1950s was suddenly being flooded with foreign buyers.

"Morres took off," remembers GianBeppe, "in 1954, thanks to the continually growing exports that brought the breath of fresh air the company needed." The hard days were about to end. In 1957, Mario received his driver's license and bought a used Fiat 1100. The previous year he had arranged for a passport in preparation for trips out of the country selling the inimitable Morres quality. "My father didn't have time to savor his success," recalls GianBeppe. "He died suddenly on Saturday, November 9, 1957, in my arms. His heart had given way under the strain of years of hard work, stress, and worry. He left to his sons a small company, but one that was theirs only, a respected name, and a product that was gaining recognition." The story of Mario finishes and that of GianBeppe abruptly begins.

5 - 5 1/2 INTERNO
6 - 6 1/2 INTERNO
- 7 1/2 INTERNO
8 - 8 1/2 INTERNO
INTERNO
INTERNO

On a windy day in early August, GianBeppe, lively and elegant in his eighties, wearing rough linen and two-tone shoes, relates how the encounter with Fronzoni happened by chance among the stands of the Vigevano shoe fair. It was Fronzoni's suggestion that the company—originally called Morres but renamed due to legal action taken by an Emilian company with the same name—take the family surname instead. GianBeppe remembers asking Fronzoni for advice about the new name.

"Simple," he said, "What is your name?"

"Moreschi," I answered.

"That will be your new name."

〰〰〰

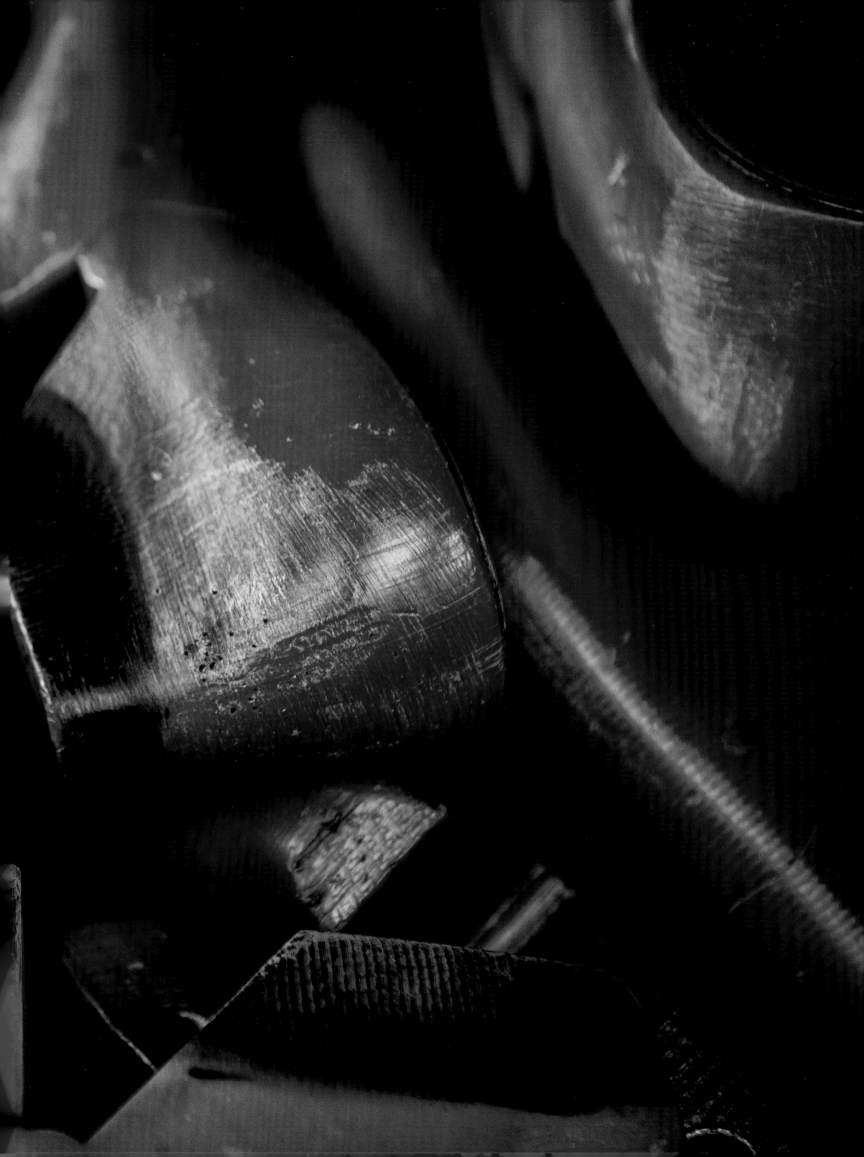

"Fronzoni also pointed out," continues GianBeppe, "that a name on its own is not enough to identify a product, and that it was necessary to mark it with a graphic symbol that, by itself, would distinguish it from others. He invented the 'M' formed by two stylized men's shoes. Black on white because, as he stated, 'they were the truest, most indelible colors.' He advised me to register the logo both in Italy and abroad and I owe him thanks for that because there have been numerous and constant attempts to copy us, with a greater or lesser degree of success." GianBeppe continues, "He explained that even if the name was illegible to the Asian world, everybody would be able to clearly recognize the logo of the shoes and associate it with the name. He was right." The encounter was governed by instinct and created a spark between two different but similarly visionary personalities. It resulted in a new start for the company as it set out on its contemporary journey, with the stamp of one of the most important names in Italian graphic design. AG Fronzoni, a clear thinker, with a gentle mien and delicate mannerisms, was a radical graphic innovator and one of the most sophisticated designers of the twentieth century. Born in Pistoia in 1923, he lived his whole life in Milan, the only Italian city, he said, in which "things happened and stimulating encounters [could] take place."

He would often say that what "a designer," as he preferred to describe himself, had to do above all was make choices, or rather, make decisions with complete awareness. For Fronzoni "choice" related to everything because "everything was part of the project." As he often reminded his students, "A project starts with designing ourselves in the way that we each live, drink, eat, dress, move around the city, and relate to other people." In his approach to design, Fronzoni aimed to combine a personal and precise vision of the world.

〰〰〰〰〰

Opposite: GBM with an ostrich hide in 1983.

"

A MAN
CANNOT MAKE A PAIR
OF SHOES RIGHTLY
UNLESS HE DO IT IN A
DEVOUT MANNER.

"

Thomas Carlyle

"His commissioner had before him a mild-mannered man but one of great clarity and strength, capable of taking forward, daring choices. For several clients Fronzoni was a beacon, a person that enabled them to make not only professional leaps, but also ethical and political ones" (Massimo Curzi, "Inventory for Authors,"*Inventario 09*, 2014, 26, Corraini edizioni). His student, Ester Mannito, recalled in the book *A Lesson with AG Fronzoni: From the Didactics of Design to the Didactics of Lifestyle* (Plugin, 2012): "Clasped under his arm were several newspapers, the handle of a black umbrella in hand. He laid the newspapers on the desk, propped the umbrella against the wall, deftly slipped off his hat and placed it on the chair. He wore loose-fitting black trousers, a black high-neck sweater, and a black cardigan with matching buttons on top. He wore a pair of black shoes that I later discovered were lace-up Polacchini (ankle boots). To begin, he greeted us with a crisp 'Good morning' that he pronounced, peering at us with a rapid and intense gaze. Then he took the chalk, turned to the blackboard, and wrote 'AG Fronzoni'. He turned back to us and said 'This is my name,' and without concerning himself with our social or cultural background, began speaking about design and its profession as though before a group of colleagues."

That "M," formed of two men's shoes coupled together to form a bold, abstract, and figurative shape, is a distinct and unmistakable symbol that should be considered as the icon that enabled the brand to stand out at a global level. The brand was registered across the world, and today, Moreschi distribution continues to expand, reaching eighty-five countries. Vigevano, due to the sorts of serendipities that are often independent of any historical-geographic cause or reliance on the resources of the area, "became, in the space of a few years, the third capital of Italy, the shoe capital," according to Lucio Mastronardi, a Vigevanese writer and author of *The Shoemaker from Vigevano* (although better known for the other volume in the trilogy on his birth town *The Teacher from Vigevano*, the subject of the film by Elio Petri and masterfully interpreted by the actor Alberto Sordi).

> " **ELEGANCE IS A STRANGE VIRUS: THOSE WHO HAVE IT NEVER GET BETTER AND THOSE WHO DON'T NEVER CATCH IT.** "

AG Fronzoni

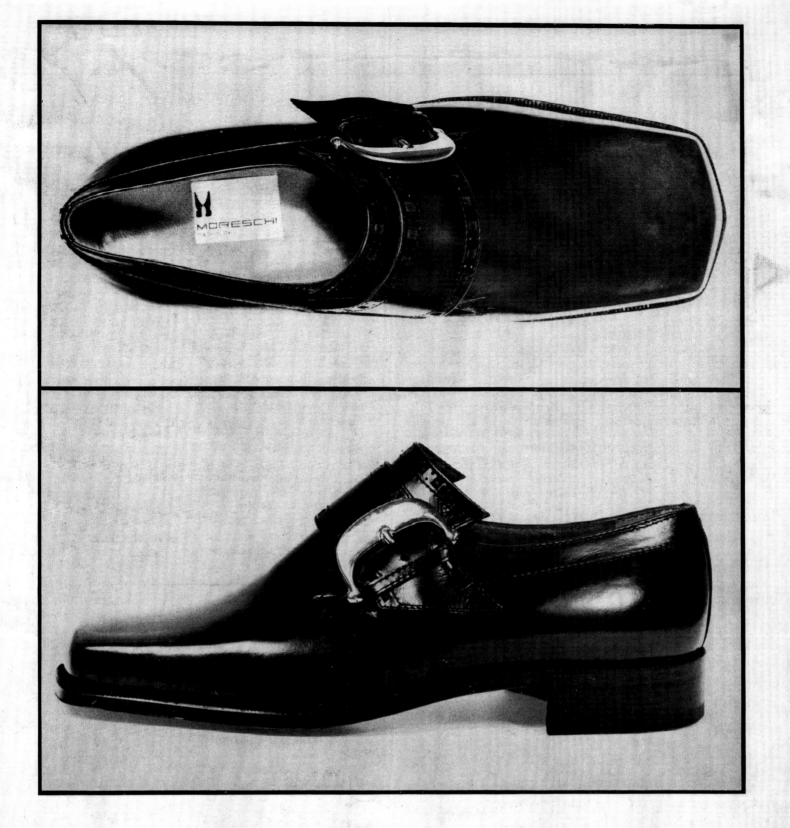

È prepotente

Non ve ne siete accorti?
È il mocassino più prepotente
che abbiamo mai visto da Moreschi:
per via di quella punta squadrata
romboidale, penetrante e possessiva.
Per il resto, è un mocassino gentile,
nel più tenero vitello anilina,
con l'alto cinturino operato
e la sua brava fibbia.
Visto di profilo, un persuasore,
visto dall'alto un dominatore.

Moreschi di Vigevano ha modellato,
per la sua collezione di calzature-protagoniste,
e di personaggi del bel calzare.

Derby!

Lo sapevamo.
Doveva venire.
E mocassini e stivaletti e pumps ...
E scarpe Blücher
(quelle che il Maresciallo
calzò la sera prima della vittoria
sul campo)
e polacchini e polacchetti
e ancora mocassini ...
Di tutti i modelli di scarpe
presentati da Moreschi
su queste nostre pagine
mancava soltanto uno,
lui,
il classico,
il superbo,
l'inimitabile.
Il modello tutto sicurezza
tutto tranquillità,
con la tomaia guarnita
da ornamentali trafori,
la mascherina
raddoppiata,
impunturata,
stringata
solidamente.
Derby!
La scarpa dell'uomo saldo e maturo.
Moreschi l'ha realizzata
in un pellame lucido
color rosso Luxor,
un rosso tra il sauro ed il roano,
vena di purosangue.

*Dalla Collezione di Calzature per Uomo
di Moreschi di Vigevano,
Autunno-Inverno 1969-1970*

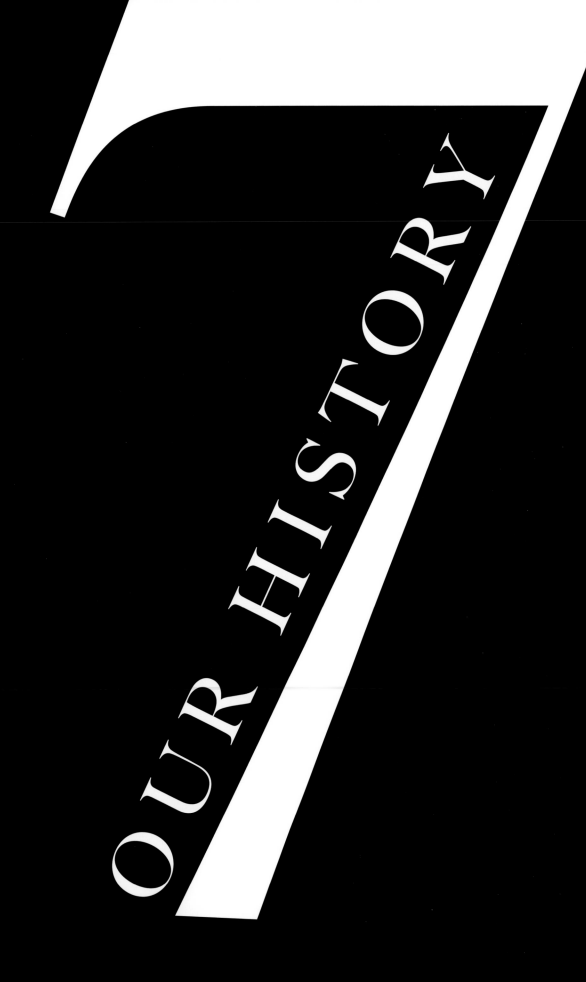

OUR HISTORY

19

40

Mario Moreschi leaves a promising
career at a bank to begin the
development of the shoe company
that would soon bear his name.

At the start of the decade, Mario Moreschi starts from scratch with the Morres shoe company.
In 1957 GianBeppe takes the helm.

19

50

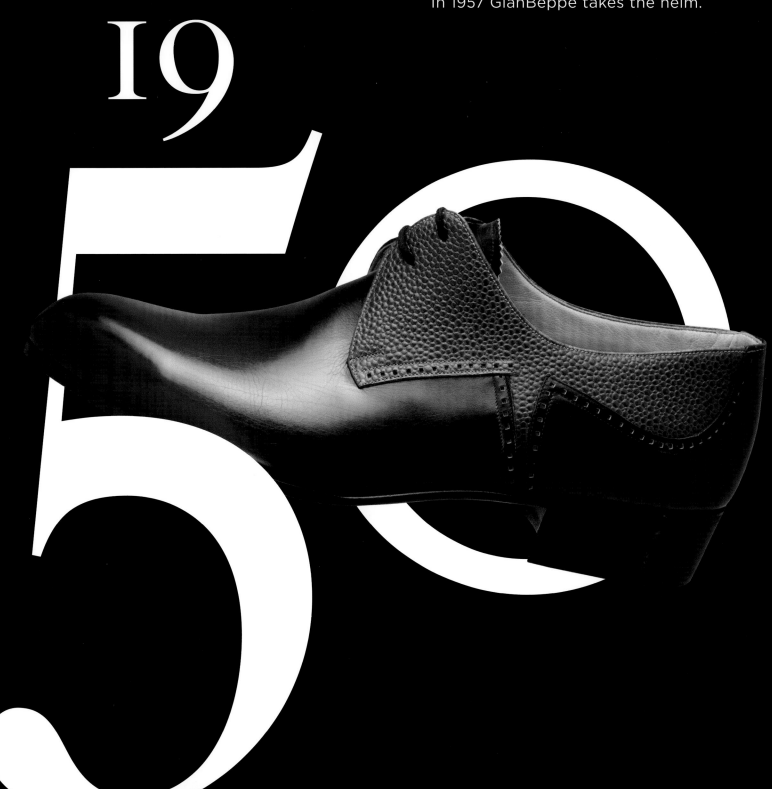

19 60

Inauguration of the new
headquarters on Via Montello
and the birth of the Moreschi brand
with its famous logo.

Moreschi opens its two Milan stores and spends the 1970s in the company of Piedo Bombetta, the company's stick-man cartoon mascot used in advertisements in the *Corriere della Sera*.

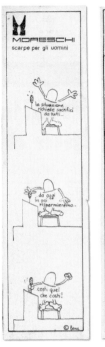

1970

51

19 88

GianBeppe Moreschi's children
begin working at the company
and the brand expands
to fifty countries across five
continents.

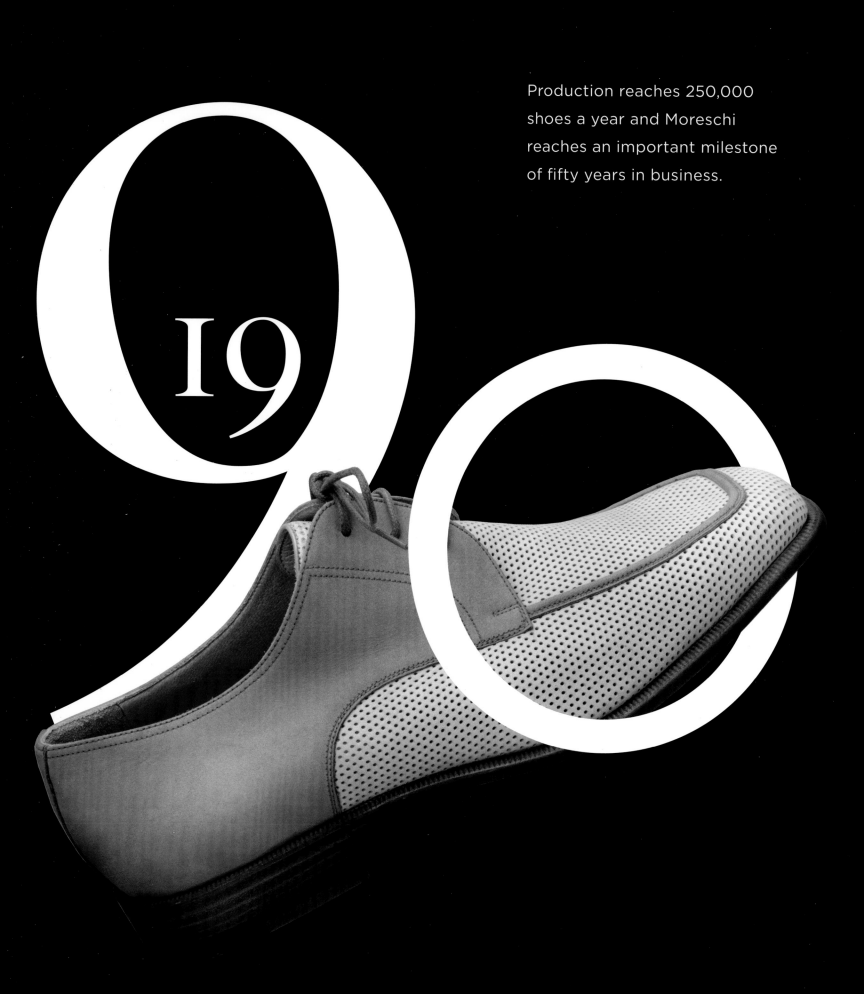

1990

Production reaches 250,000 shoes a year and Moreschi reaches an important milestone of fifty years in business.

The new 70,000-square-meter Moreschi production complex, with its large outdoor green expanse complete with small lake, welcomes employees.

Moreschi opens the boutique on Piazza San Babila and production reaches 50,000 leather garments a year.

The Moreschi production center currently occupies an area of 18,000 square meters and employs 400 people. It is the result of progressive enlargement and restructuring, overseen by GianBeppe Moreschi, who aimed to make it ever more pleasant. "Working is hard enough," he remarks. "If it becomes oppressive, people just wait for the evening so they can get out. The place of work must be a well-lit, spacious, and airy environment that testifies to the highest care for human capital, the most important resource in the creation of a high-quality, artisanal product.

"I have a nice house," he continues, "but I spend most of my time here in the factory and therefore I try to make the best of it. I'm in the office every day, I don't know what to do otherwise. I only spend two weeks a year on holiday." He receives visitors in his office, furnished with an armchair and tufted leather sofa, sitting behind a light wooden desk. There is a television on a stool and in front, in a row, are three small silver-plated, floral ceramic shoes. Beside the desk there is a globe. It could be seen as a symbol of the expansion of the family company to the international market. GianBeppe takes satisfaction in narrating the story of his adventurous father and the birth of the company. He delights in the smaller things, remembering faithful collaborators and reciting anecdotes. He is the living memory of the company. From his account emerges a respect for the employees who constitute the wealth of the company.

The factory, inaugurated in 2003, is a clean, exemplary construction in the form of a parallelepiped of 180 x 74 x 10 meters that was intended by GianBeppe to resemble a shoebox. The exterior is constructed of white cement blocks marked with fine black lines that delimit the perimeter. At the center, the entrance block is made entirely of glass. The front area contains offices, while the rest of the structure is dedicated to production. It was designed by Professor Mario Bonzanini, who designed for Moreschi from 1955 to 2000, including private projects, and established a close relationship with the family. Inside, the atmosphere of hushed concentration gives it the air of a cathedral. Everything is clean and orderly: work stations are in line; the floor is spick-and-span; movements are precise and rhythmic. The dusky leather storeroom is the pride of the company and has the sacred feel of a cellar full of vintage wines. Amid the low hum of sewing machines, seamsters in white overalls pull the double stitches of the seaming in regular movements, as precisely as surgeons. The work is steady but not rushed, displaying the calm employment of a manual expertise developed through constant practice.

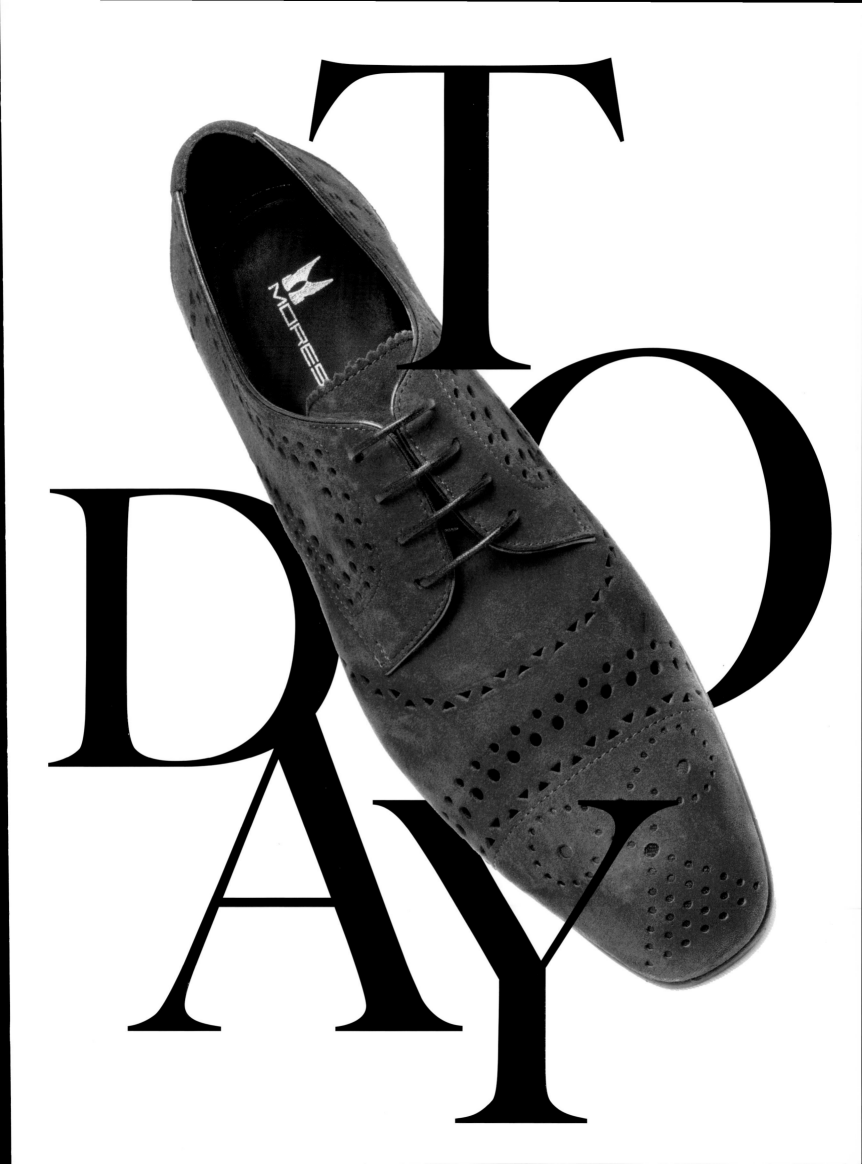

THE
TREASURE ROOM

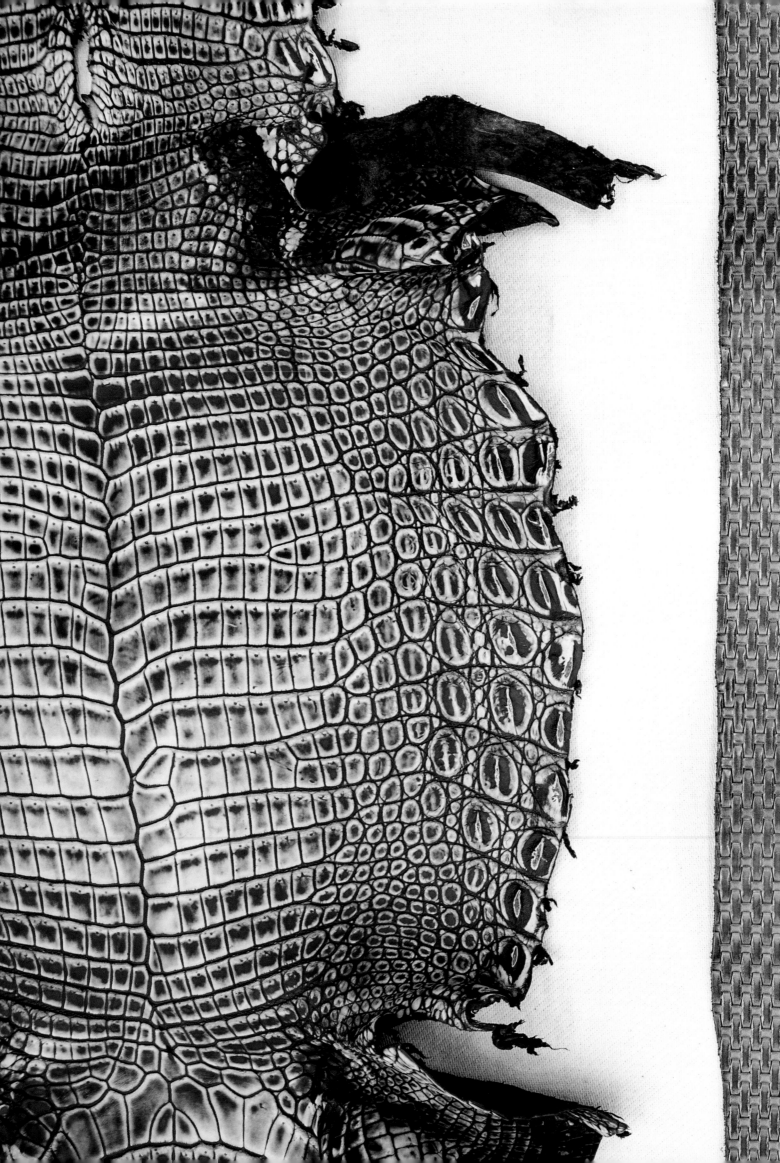

EVERY STRIP
OF LEATHER IS SPECIAL.
OVER TIME
IT ACQUIRES A PATINA
THAT REFLECTS ITS
LIFE AND STRENGTHENS
ITS CHARACTER.

The leather store is located on the first floor of the building in a cool, dark space similar to a vintage wine cellar. Indeed, alongside the leathers, are select aged bottles of third-generation wine belonging to Mario Moreschi, who now manages the company together with his brothers, Stefano and Francesco. It is the safe of the company. Here lies the treasured range of select leather that ensures the quality of the shoes is maintained. Special attention is dedicated to the leathers. Female backs, tied in packs, are ordered and hung. Prized vintages are marked and rest on shelves. There is even a selection from 1946 that belonged to the grandfather, Mario Moreschi. Like wine, leather improves with time, and therefore it pays to build up a reserve. In the Moreschi store there are back-up supplies to last at least six months. The leather for soles are vegetable-tanned with extracts of chestnut tannin and mimosa.

The grandson Mario explains that the leather trade is concentrated in the hands of a few wholesalers that buy the hides at auction and supply them to the tanneries. The manufacturers buy from the tanneries, situated for the most part in Arzignano in Veneto, Santa Croce sull'Arno in Tuscany, and Turbigo in Lombardy. Moreschi uses local tanneries, demonstrating a particular loyalty to the shoemaking district.

In the hide storeroom, the skins are packed and ordered by type on shelves, as if in a library: nappa, suede, calf, crocodile, ostrich, lizard, and python. The great variety speaks to one of the distinctive characteristics of Moreschi, known internationally for two-tone shoes and the capacity to pull off difficult pairings such as suede and alligator. The average quantity deposited is enough for a year's production.

According to Mario, the origins of the hides vary: caiman arrives from Colombia and crocodile from Louisiana, deer and peccary from North America. Goat comes from Nigeria and kangaroo from Australia, while China provides the goat skins for linings. France provides calf, while hides from medium-sized calves come from the East. Bull, small oxen, and cow are sourced from Germany, Holland, and Denmark. Goat and lamb hides are used in the main for linings.

The use of prized leather has always been a distinctive characteristic of Moreschi, which adheres firmly to the international laws regulating its use: all footwear produced with high-quality materials is accompanied with CITES certification attesting to its origin and legality. The rich endowment of hides, cataloged and arranged by type, is testimony not only to the expert knowledge behind their selection, treatment, and usage, but also to the hallmark style of the brand. Aside from their tapered form, the mark of Moreschi shoes lies in the variety of leathers used and the search for unexpected pairings of color and type.

Lively color is also glimpsed in the men's collections that make daring use of unusual tonalities, often coupled with reptile vamps.

"
THE SMELL
OF HIDE AND LEATHER
IS A MARK OF ITS QUALITY.
A DEEP AND MASCULINE
SCENT.
"

GianBeppe Moreschi

> **"**
> ## I HAVE
> ## THE SIMPLEST TASTES.
> ## I AM ALWAYS SATISFIED
> ## WITH THE BEST.
> **"**

Oscar Wilde

" A MAN BECOMES RICH;
HE IS BORN ELEGANT. "

Honoré de Balzac

Even before entering the leather storeroom, the character of the brand can be appreciated from the broad, light entrance to the headquarters—a parallelepiped of 18,000 square meters set within 70,000 square meters of parkland. Traditional work benches have been placed beside the window front of the entrance: one with old wooden shoe forms and various tools; one with cardboard outlines for uppers, cutting knives, and pieces of leather; and a final one with an old sewing machine and an old hand pantograph. These "relics" of craftwork testify to the deep respect for tradition on which the excellence of the brand has been built. The corridors contain glass cases housing iconic models to convey to the hurried visitor the history of the company and the stages in its evolution. The first impression is one of resolute modernity. In the big "white box," 400 people work to produce over 250,000 pairs of shoes a year. A visit to the factory reveals the consideration for the importance of the workplace and the special attention given to the comfort of workers. The orderliness is thorough. On the spotless pavement, yellow stripes mark out routes: one for pedestrians, one for bicycles (also yellow), and one for trolleys. There are no scraps or leftover cuttings on the floor; everything has its place. Nothing is left to disturb the perfect parallel lines of the production chains.

" EVERY SHOE, A WALK,
EVERY WALK,
A DIFFERENT CONCEPTION
OF THE WORLD. "

Nanni Moretti

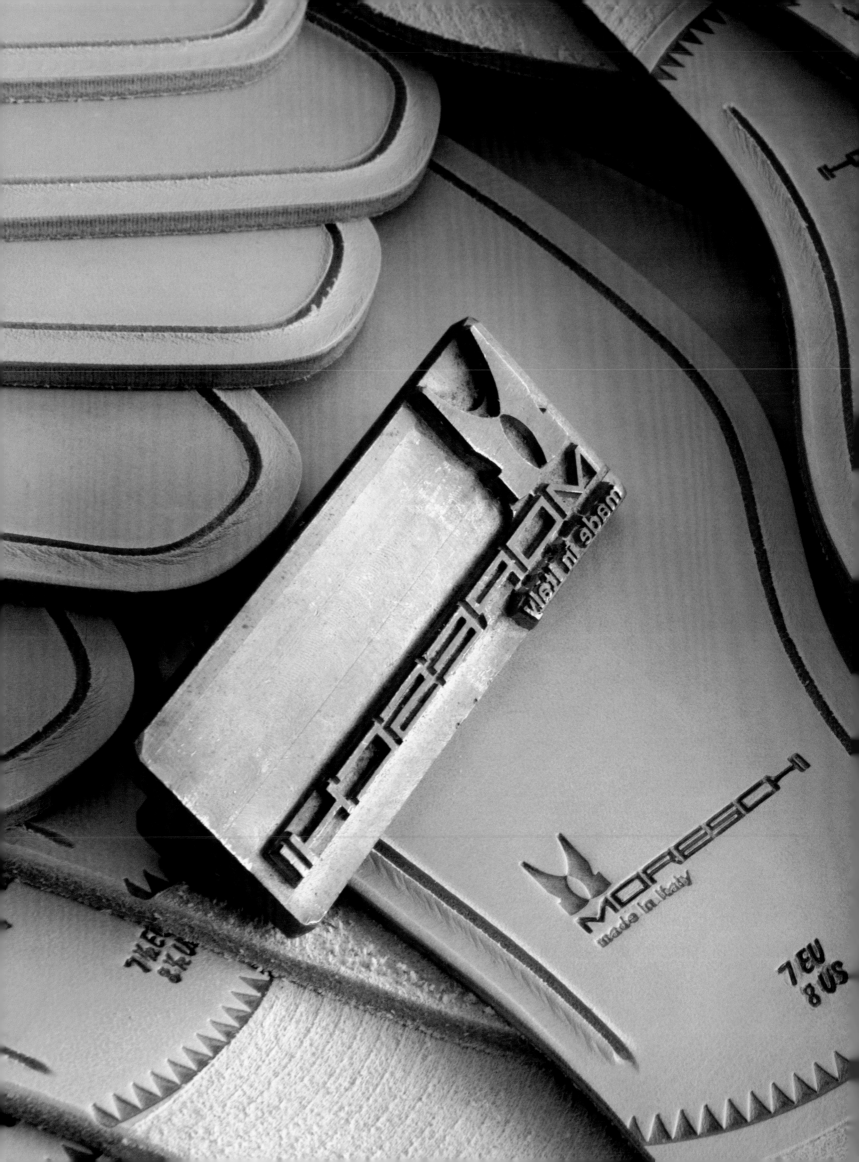

The movements of the workers, all in white overalls, are rhythmic and precise. Seamsters manually stitch the uppers with two needles, moving their hands as if engaged in some ritual dance. It takes 250 to 300 steps to make a shoe. The process begins in the modeling department where models are created on wooden forms, reflecting fifty years of history. The cutting department is as autonomous and organized as a shoe sole factory, producing soles, insoles, and heel taps. Next is the leather-cutting, carried out so that only the best parts are used, with the consequent discarding of more than a third of the leather as offcuts and scraps. Then the preparation for the uppers: a stylist writes notes on the plastic shells. The design is applied to a fabric sheet, which is broken down into pieces and supplies instructions to the computer. A pair of uppers is composed of a minimum of eight to a maximum of twenty-four pieces of leather, cut and sewn according to precise criteria. The final step is the most complex and accounts for almost 50 percent of workers in the high-quality production team. Many years are needed to train a skilled laster: the best school is always the factory.

In the assembly phase, the upper is modeled onto the shoe form and the shoe assumes its definitive shape. This is only the halfway point. To finish the shoe, a further ten operations are required, such as the gluing and stitching of the sole to the shoe, and the finishing that, after a thorough cleaning, involves applying polish, brushing, and inserting the leather insole with its woven black-on-white label into the shoe. Then there are the final touches and coloring before the final check. The last step is boxing: like precious jewels, the shoes are placed in boxes and wrapped carefully in tissue paper.

Opposite: A Moreschi shoemaker's work table.

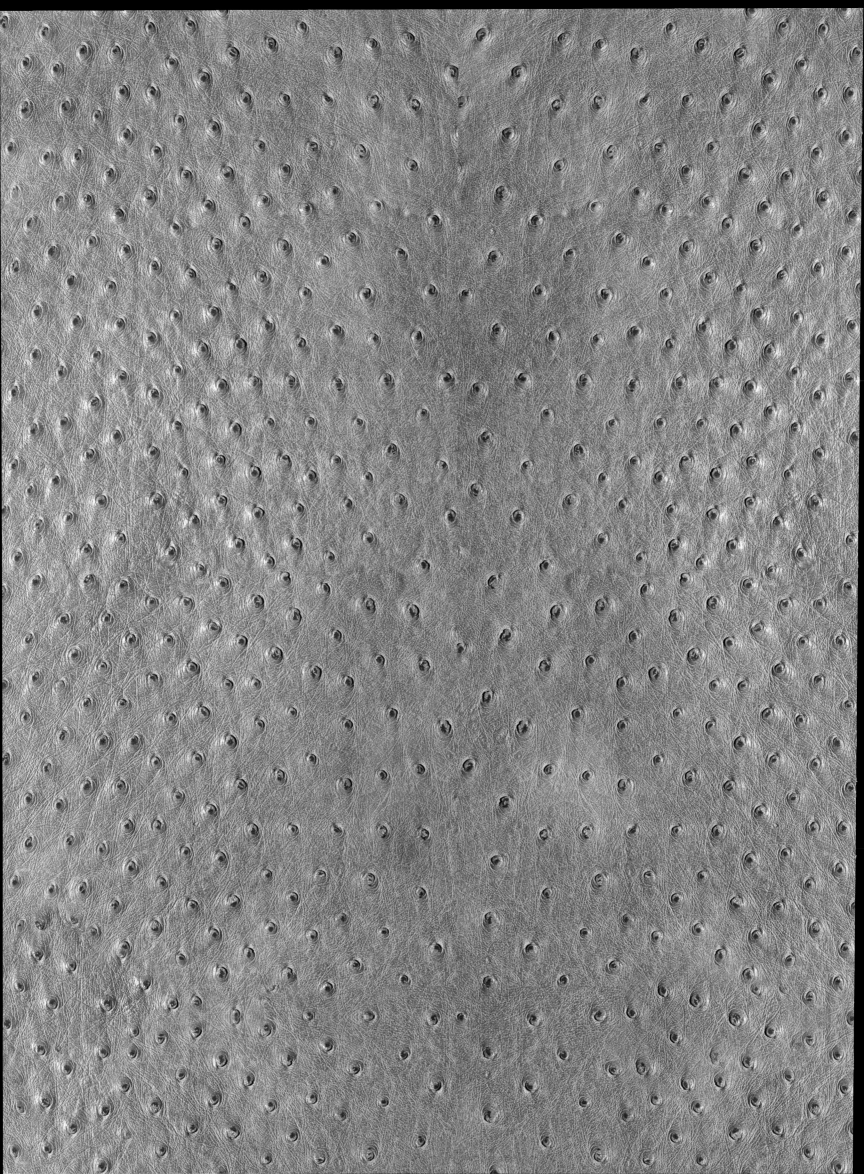

〰〰〰〰

Opposite: Ostrich leather.

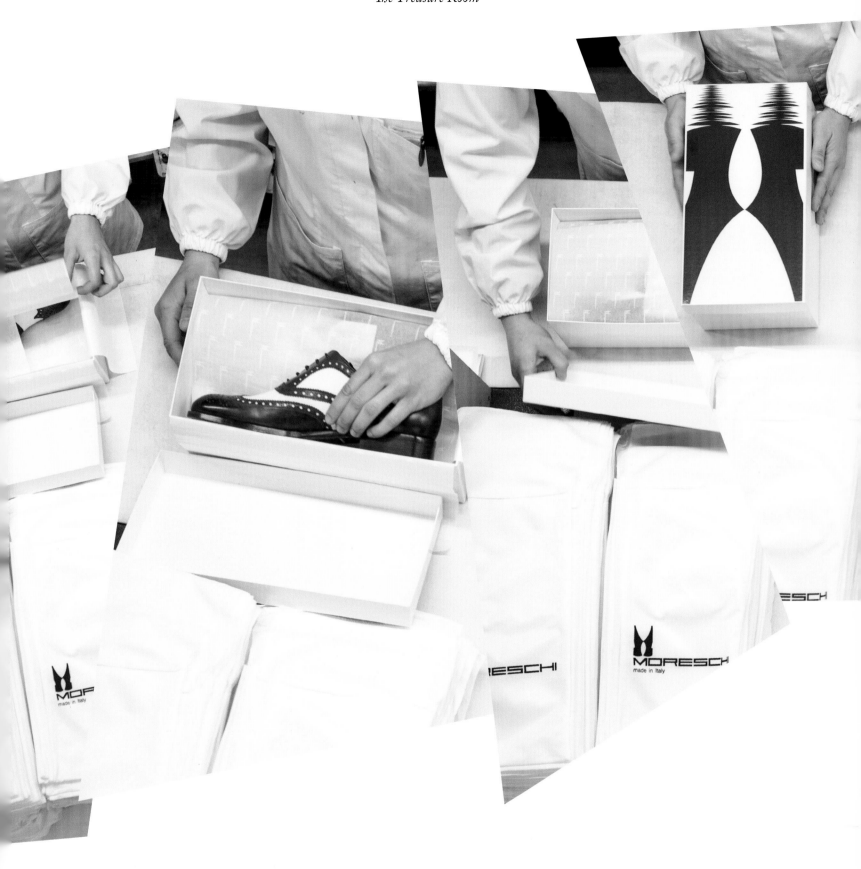

CLASSIC
ELEGANCE

" **HAPPINESS,
LIKE A FINE WINE,
SHOULD BE SAVORED
SIP BY SIP.** "

Ludwig Feuerbach

An appreciation for the good life is a quality that has been passed down from father to child and that has, in certain ways, influenced production. Standing as testament is the Moreschi 1946 Guado al Tasso Limited Edition design, launched with the Marquis Piero Antinori. Mario Moreschi, a bon vivant with a passion for good wine and healthy food, explains the story in detail. One of the diamonds of the Moreschi collection is the handcrafted Francesine lace-up, hand-dubbed with *vinacce* (the residue from crushed grape skins) from Guado al Tasso. Owned by the Marquis Antinori, this historic Tuscan wine estate is located in Bolgheri.

The combination may seem strange, but it is based on certain similarities between these high-quality producers. Just as leather is stocked and aged in a dark, damp storeroom, so too the wines of Guado al Tasso are matured in barrels in an underground cellar, kept at the right level of constant humidity in order to bring about the optimal process of refinement.

The union of these two historic Made in Italy emblems originated with Mario Moreschi's passion for the world of wine. "In November 2012," recounts Mario, "during a tasting session of Cervaro della Sala at Castello della Sala in Umbria, I met the Marquis Piero Antinori and we outlined an idea that then became the design for the first pair of shoes dyed by hand with grape skins from Guado al Tasso, an estate that produces wine for oenophiles."

There are 120 pairs of shoes in the Moreschi Guado al Tasso line. Each pair is unique and sold together with a 2011 magnum of the precious wine in a gorgeous box containing a book of the history of the Tuscan wine estate and an invitation from the Antinori family to spend two days among the Bolghieri vineyards.

The shoes are made with full-grain calfskin, aged for over thirty-six months. The upper is hand-dyed through a special procedure that uses aniline and grape skins to re-create in the shoe the same color and hues of the dark purple wine.

The Moreschi shoes dyed with Guado al Tasso grape skins seal the union between these two examples of Italian excellence, and testify to their commitment to entrepreneurialism informed by heritage—a heritage that blends innovation with the added value of a territorial belonging, which is instrumental in making so many "Made in Italy" products the icons they are.

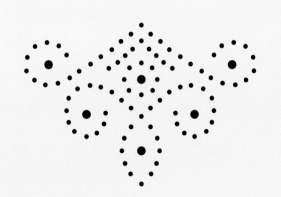

ANATOMY OF A
STYLE

TO DEFINE THE AESTHETIC
OF A MORESCHI SHOE
IT IS NECESSARY TO SHARPEN
SIGHT AND TOUCH TO
APPRECIATE THE ACCURACY
OF ARTISANAL WORKMANSHIP
AND THE VARIETY
OF LEATHERS.

SFILATO

FORMA   162

SIZE   7- 7/

OPER.   PAOLO

ANTISCIVOLO

FILO 40 +
SALPA IMBOTT.
RIPORTO 7mm

RIPIEGATO

ART.   A547

FORMA

SIZE

OPER.

ANTIS

FILO
SPER

7- 7/

NDREA

SUO

A A
MAR

SFILATO

ITALIA   ROMANA   GERMANIA   ifaba.it

51
52
53
54
55
56
57
58
59
60

⬤⦂⬤⦂⬤⦂⬤

To describe the Moreschi style, it is necessary to study the preboxed shoes leaving the production line, and to get to know them. First, touch must be refined in order to recognize the variety of leathers that are the pride of the brand, and to examine the different constructions and varied forms of the shoes, characterized by a rich repertoire of models. A glossary of models illustrating the range of shoes produced has been assembled at the company, in addition to a brief anatomy of shoes: toe cap (can be decorated), vamp, eyelet stay, quarters, and counter.

This chapter describes details of the workmanship on the upper, from the edge, to the perforations, to the flower. Then there are the stitches, from those done by machine, to those pinched, to those done by hand and their various types—from turning, to sewing the hem, to the edging.

Robustness and impermeability are ensured through "Goodyear" construction: a welt is sewn directly to the upper and the insole. Meanwhile the "Blake" construction method, which provides strength and resistance, is characterized by the special stitching that binds the upper to the sole. Distinctive features include the braid stitching, also known as "Tirolese" stitching, that binds the upper to the insole between the upper and the midsole, both completed entirely by hand.

〰〰〰

Opposite: A work table from the Moreschi
modeling room.

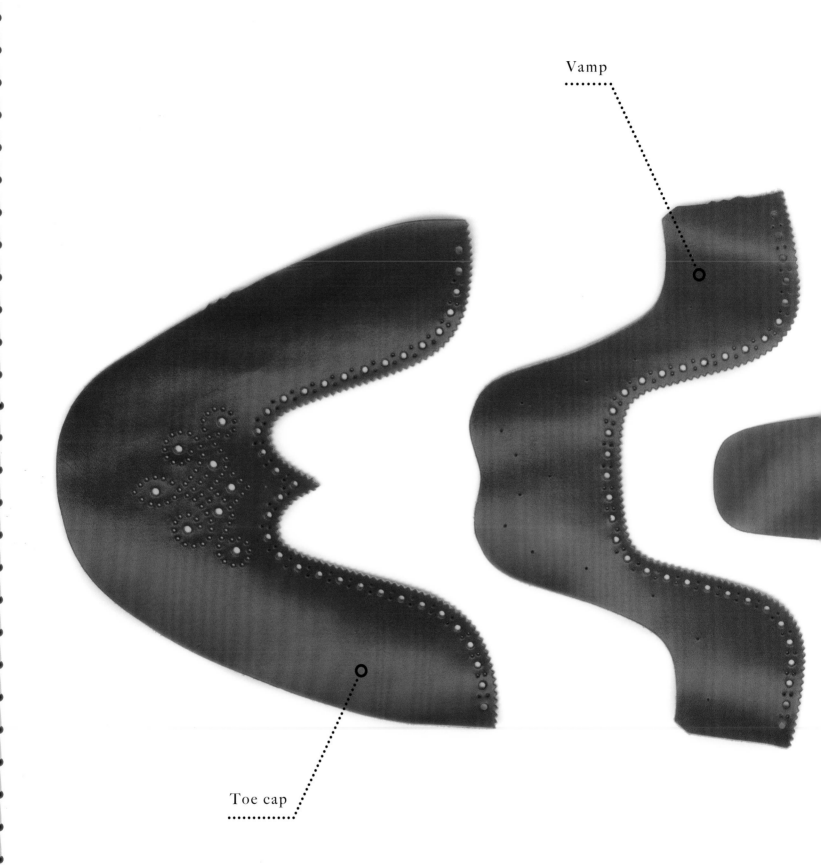

Vamp

Toe cap

150

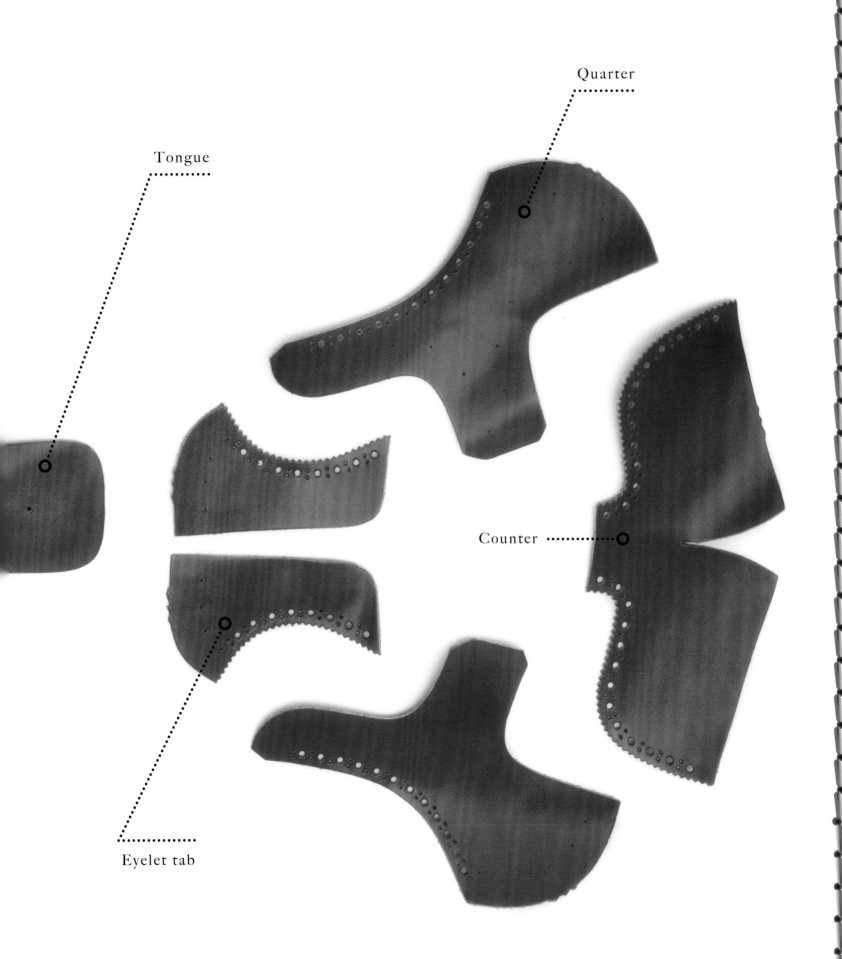

Quarter

Tongue

Counter

Eyelet tab

151

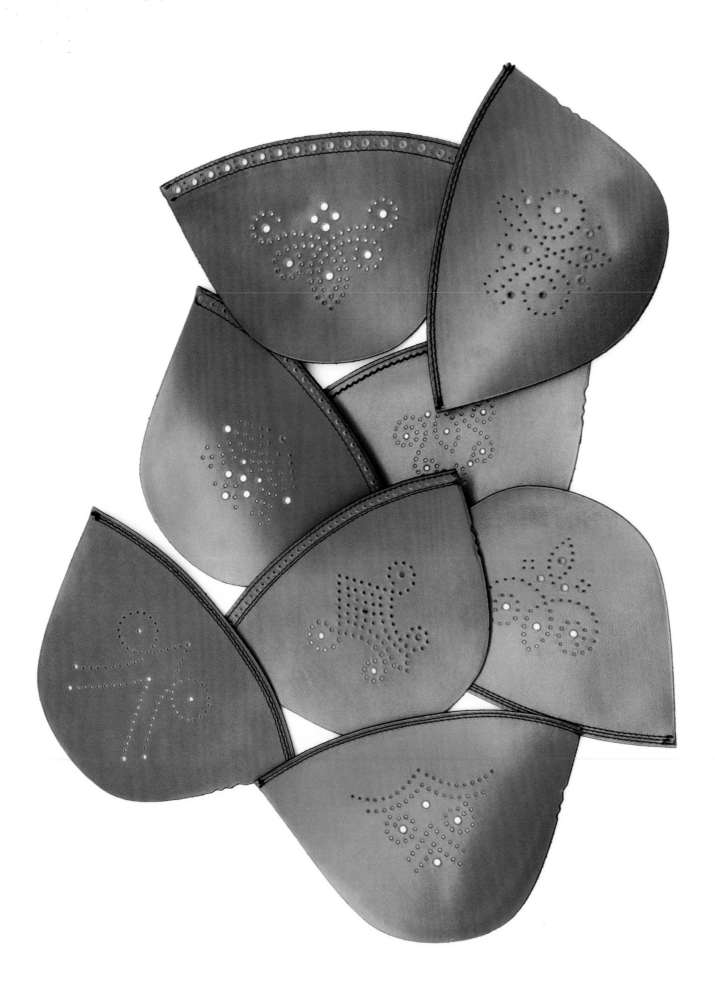

152

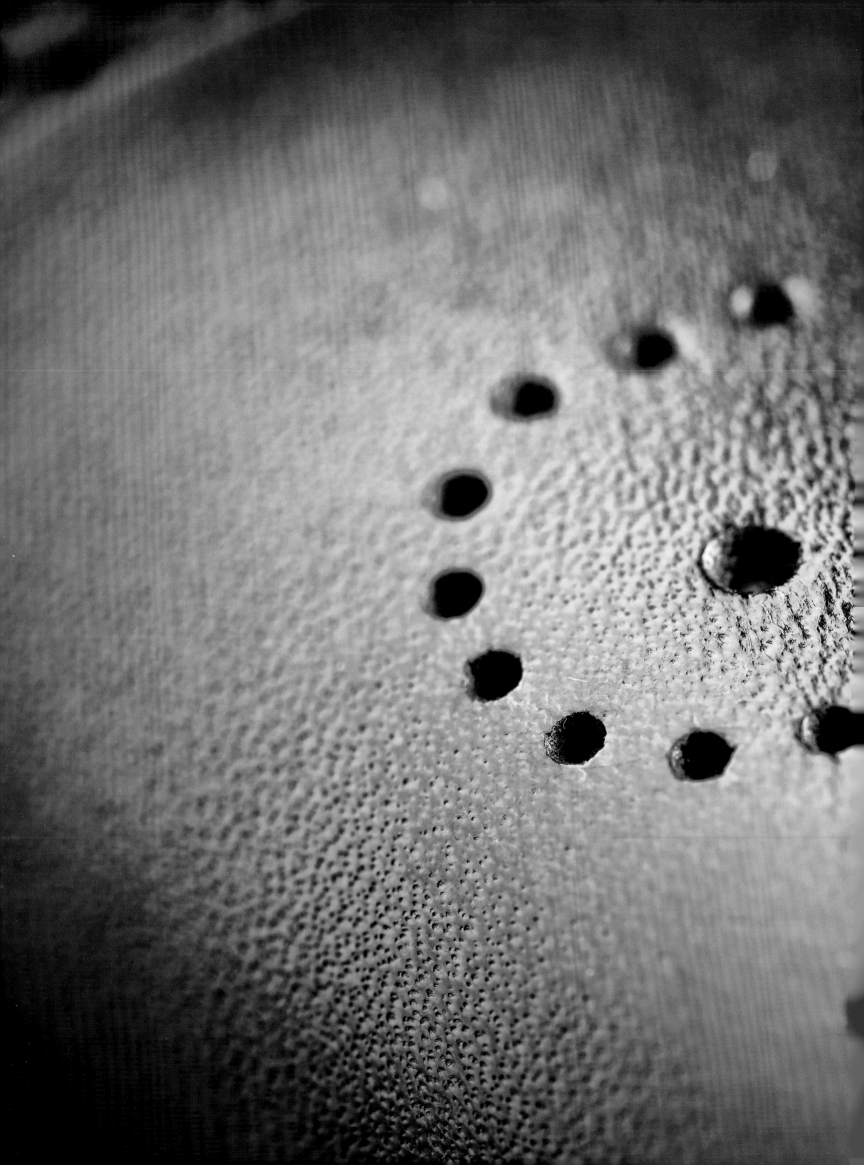

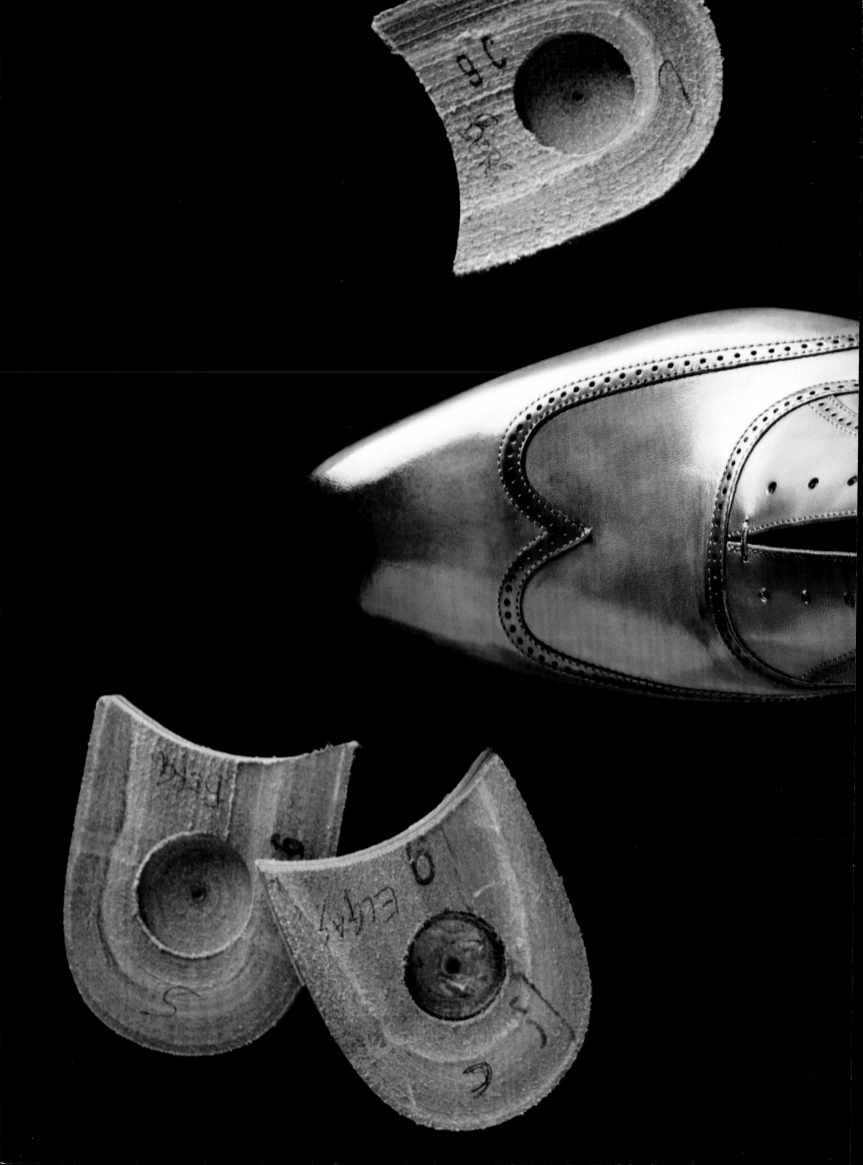

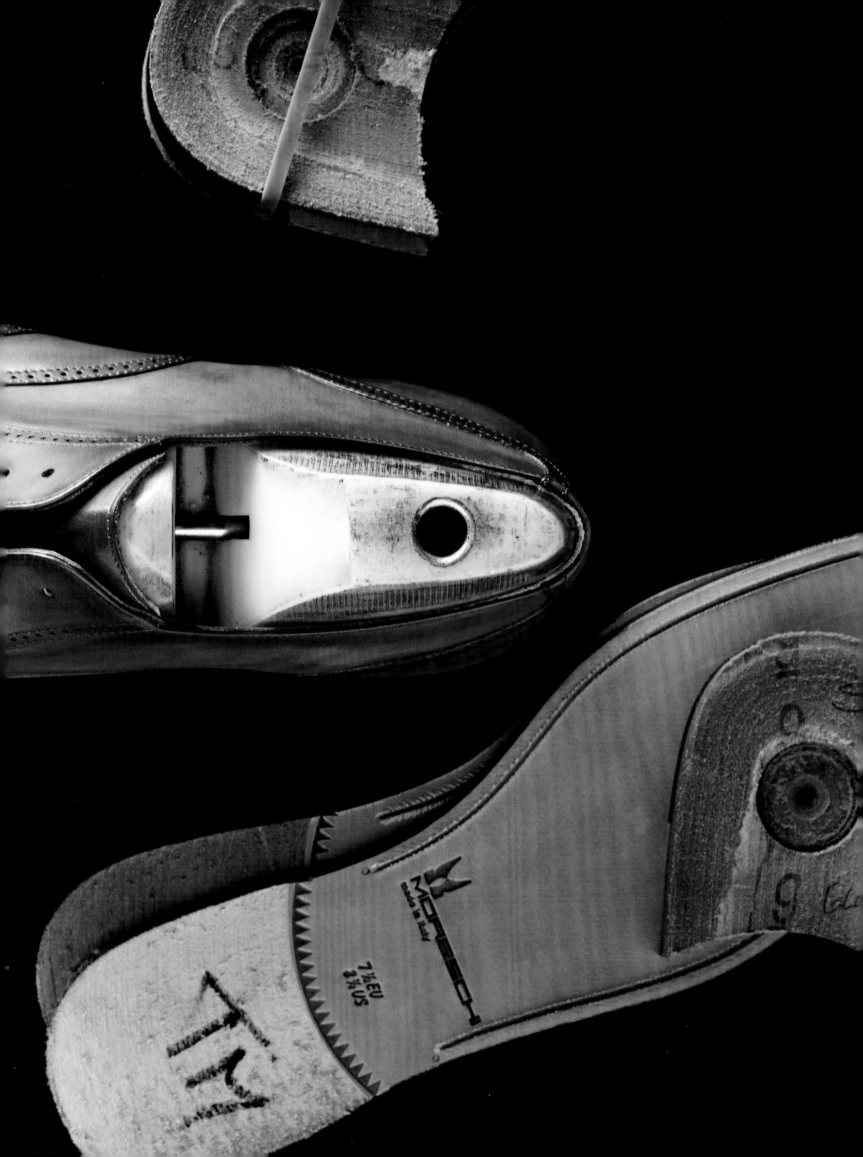

TUBULAR CONSTRUCTION ON FORM

BLAKE CONSTRUCTION

GOODYEAR CONSTRUCTION

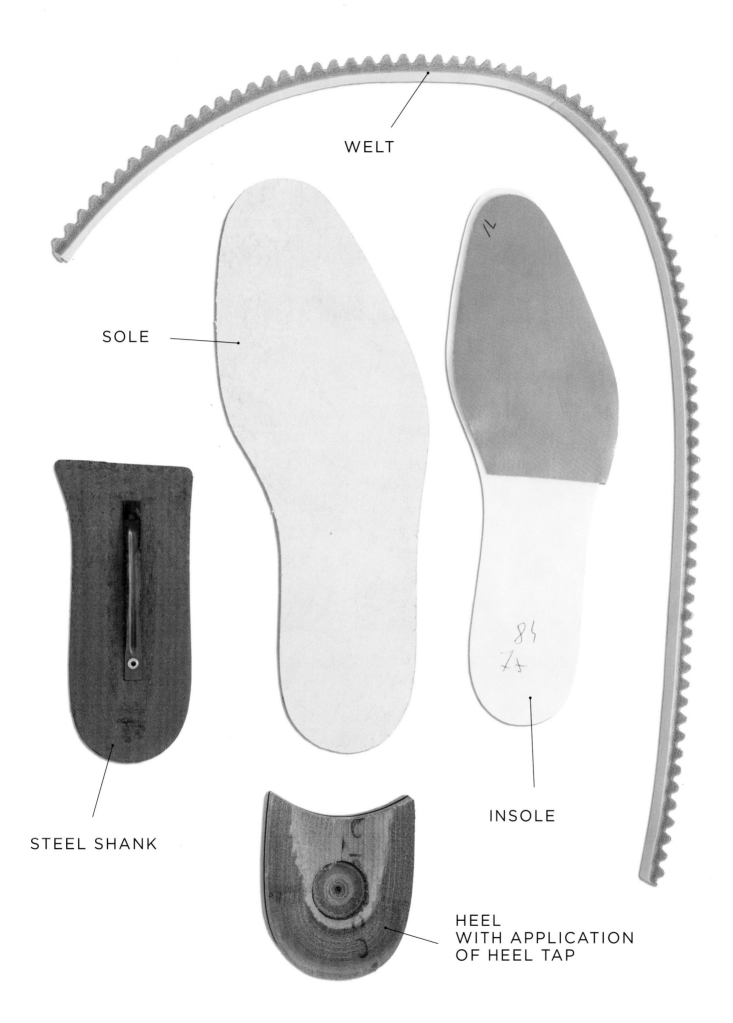

WELT

SOLE

INSOLE

STEEL SHANK

HEEL
WITH APPLICATION
OF HEEL TAP

250 000 PAIRS

85 COUNTRIES IN THE WORLD

2003 NEW FACTORY

400 EMPLOYEES

500 sq m NURSERY

70 000 sq m FLOOR SPACE

18 000 sq m INTERNAL SPACE COMPANY

MIN **250** PRODUCTION STEPS

MAX **350**

LEATHER FOR SOLES USED IN A YEAR **120.000 KG**

STITCHES ON UPPER **500**

50.000 LEATHER PIECES

140 km OF STRING USED PER YEAR

END CLIENT NATIONALITIES **145**

365 DAYS AGING TIME OF LEATHER FOR SOLES

1.000.000 SQUARE FEET OF LEATHER USED IN A YEAR

The tubular loafer is very flexible and is stitched entirely by hand on the form using two needles. The "Guanto" production method enables the upper to mold itself like a glove to the form of the foot, giving freedom of movement. The "driver" shoe is built like a loafer but the sole is a rubber insert, stitched underneath the upper. The rich collection includes oxfords; derbies; single and double monk-strap shoes; classic slippers in different varieties; stitched slip-ons, also in different varieties; tubular loafers, simple versions or variants (wide strip or tassel); basic drivers with strips, laces, or perforated; classic ankle boots with elastics, as lace-ups, or with buckles; jodhpur boots with laces or zips; trappeurs; boots; dress sneakers; casual sneakers; sandals (braided, in European varieties, and for rich Arab clientele); and bedroom slippers. Inside every shoe is a code with the article number, the form, the size, and the production number.

The glossary shows how the Moreschi men's shoe obeys precise rules, codified from tradition and experience and which, as a large part of the shoe construction is manual, is entrusted to the expert manual workers whose skills have been developed at the factory. Nothing is left to chance; rather, every step is the fruit of a tradition cultivated with passion and skill.

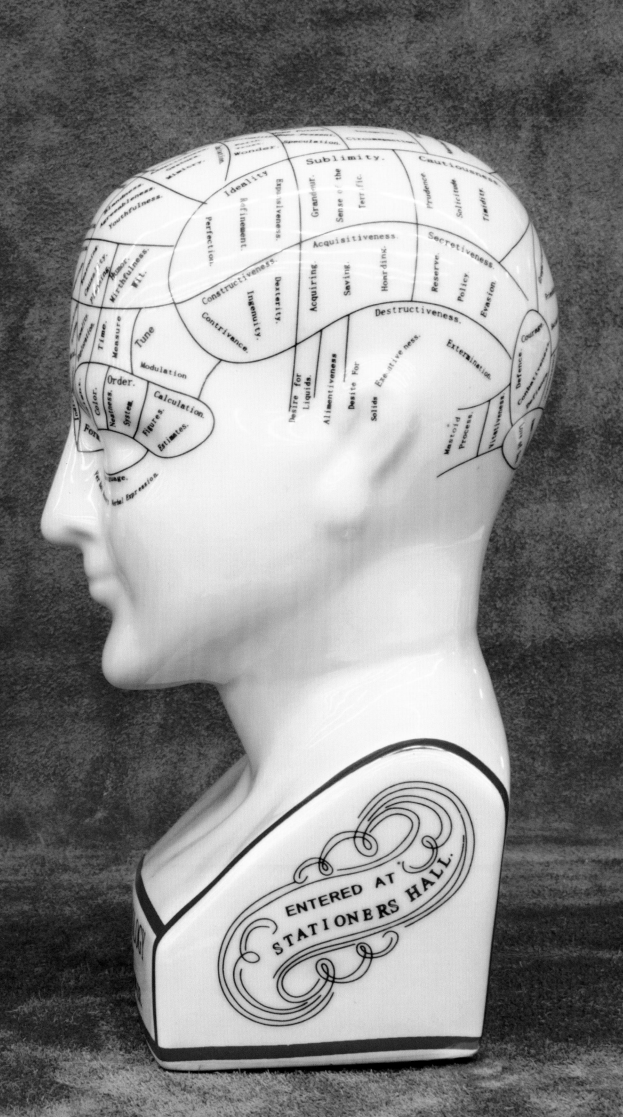

If the rules are precise and codified, where is distinctive character to be found? Above all, it lies in the adaptation of the rules of traditional construction, which guarantees strength and resistance, to contemporary variants of classic models. And it depends on the quality and variety of the skins.

GianBeppe has a wealth of anecdotes about Moreschi "quality." He tells the story of a client who, following a factory visit, declared that he had begun to take better care of his shoes after seeing how much work went into making them. Or a jet pilot who arrived at a fair with a bag containing a pair of ankle boots in double nappa that he wanted to restore, as their softness aided his piloting. Or the pianist Maurizio Pollini, who usually wore soft, black goatskin elegant shoes, and would take home ten pairs at a time. He takes satisfaction from the memory of a client who said: "To buy a pair of Moreschis is to buy seventy years of history." Then there was the person who maintained that the shoes' defects were their excessive lifespan and comfort, which discouraged changing shoes even after having worn them for a whole day. He cites a Swiss journalist who defined the company production method as "watchmaking in leather." And he refers to the advice of Thomas Bata who, after visiting the factory twice, suggested that "to improve, it would be useful not to change anything." Or the time when the band Modern Talking made an album and put a Moreschi shoe on the cover. Finally, he proudly pulls out a cover from the *Sunday Times*, May 11, 2014, that shows Gopi Hinduja, at the top of the *Times*' list of richest people in Britain, wearing a pair of Moreschi loafers. Even the success of a meeting between Sunil Mittal, the Punjabi billionaire, and the Sheikh of Kuwait was linked to Moreschi shoes. Despite their cultural differences, realizing they were wearing the same pair of shoes signed by Moreschi immediately broke the ice during the conclusion of an important deal.

It is reasonable to attribute the signature style of Moreschi to the imagination and freedom in the use of leathers, to their daring combinations, both in terms of color and grain. Many models are two-tone or dual-material, playing off sharp contrasts or unusual couplings such as suede and ostrich or crocodile. It is precisely where room for maneuver is restricted that inventiveness, skill, and quality emerge. The ergonomics deserve a special note: strength and resilience combine with lightness and elegance, signifying a particular shrewdness in construction, which is designed to offer flexibility and comfort.

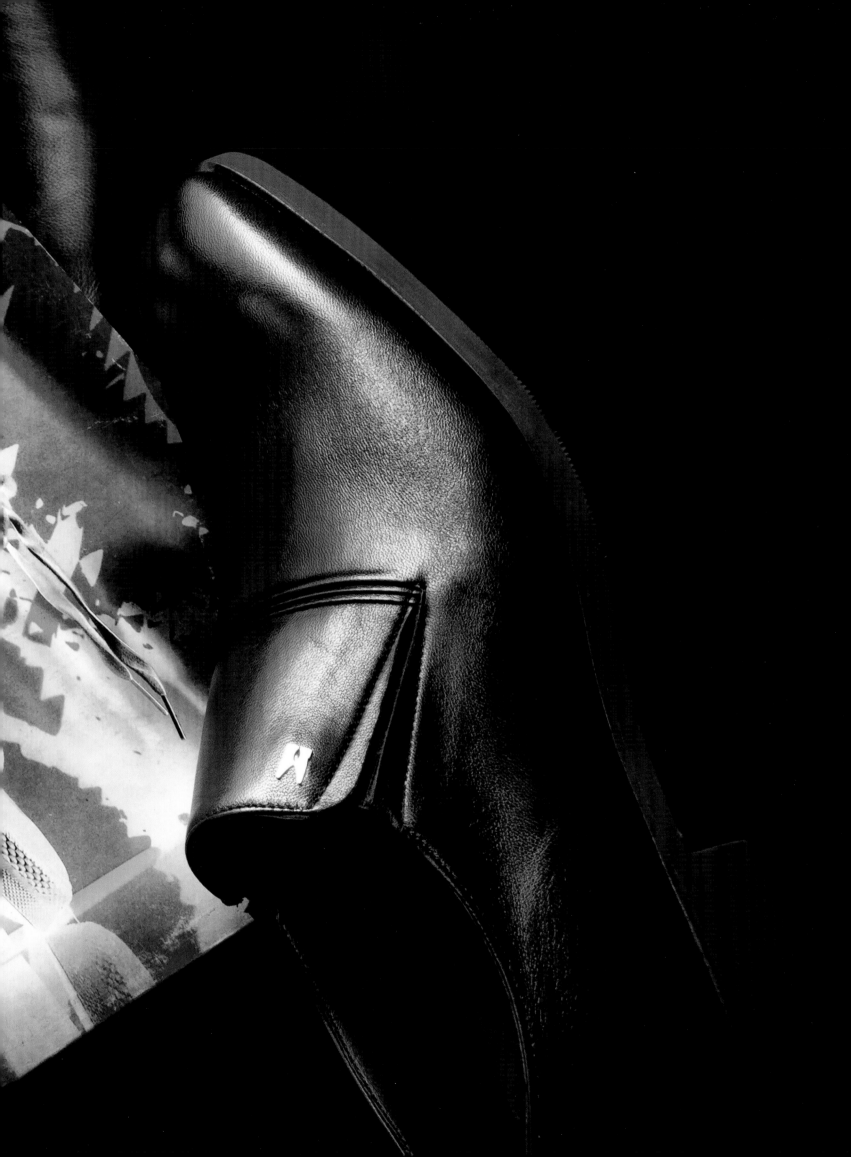

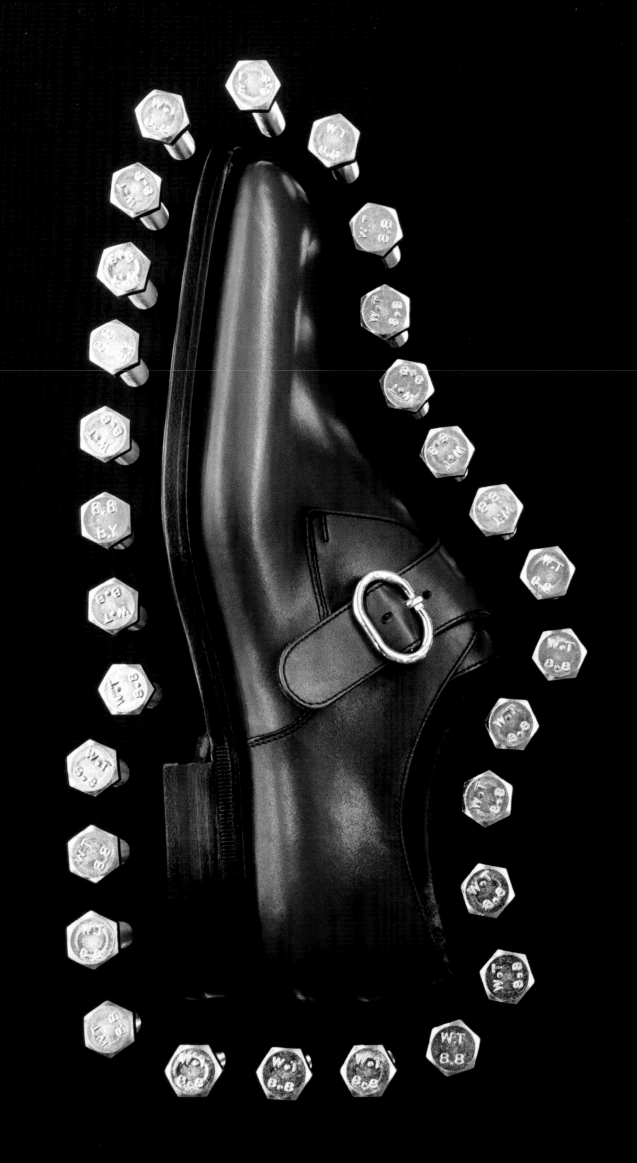

The heart of production is, and remains, men's shoes, but the expansion to national and international markets required a widening of the product range to strengthen the brand identity and place it alongside other brands. A number of men's leather items, distinguished by the quality and variety of materials used, have been introduced, along with a line of women's accessories that respond to the latest trends while respecting an established identity founded on traditional handmade methods, high quality, and a unique variety of materials.

" GIVE A GIRL
THE RIGHT SHOES,
AND SHE CAN CONQUER
THE WORLD. "

Marilyn Monroe

The range of the latest collections, especially spring and summer 2015, reveals both an imaginative approach and abundant freedom in the use of colors and combinations, including classic men's shoes with tapered lines in a rare sky blue–toned patina; and variations on the slipper with a rounded point and unexpected perforated motifs. Large perforations decorate the classic, slim, contoured Francesina lace-up. Loafers are made with woven leather and are offered in a range of dusty blues; in the suede version they are adorned with a looped silk chord and tassels.

The women's collection, for both shoes and bags, plays on themes taken from men's fabrics, such as stripes and houndstooth. Color dominates in bold tones such as fuchsia and turquoise green. Rare skins such as snake are utilized in multicolored versions with many special effects. Enlarged perforations, typical of men's shoes, highlight the profile of women's sandals, giving them an innovative look.

" COLORS, LIKE
FEATURES,
FOLLOW THE CHANGES
OF EMOTIONS. "

Pablo Picasso

SPECIAL
COLLABORATIONS

COLLABORATIONS
WITH OTHER COMPANIES
ARE BORN
OF THE NEED
FOR A COORDINATED
EFFORT
IN ORDER TO SPREAD
AN ITALIAN WAY
FOUNDED ON THE VALUES
OF TRADITION
AND INNOVATION.

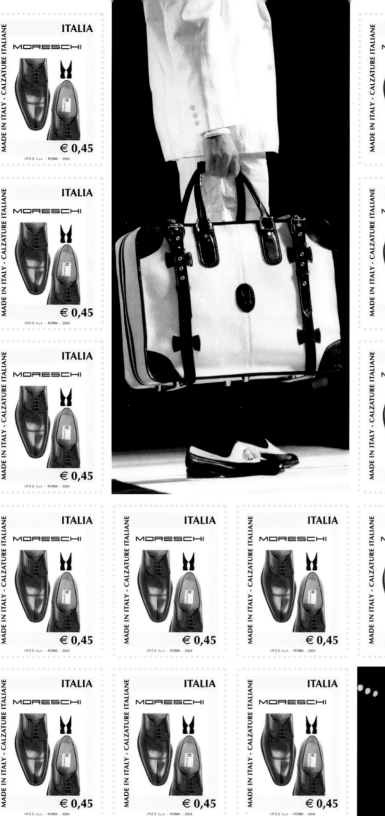

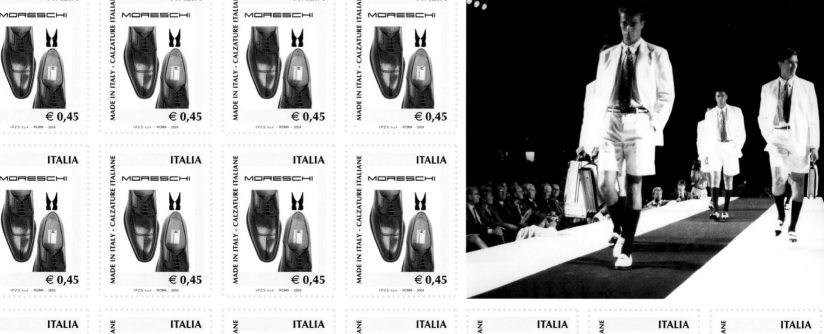

An ambassador for Made in Italy excellence, Moreschi is aware of the need for a coordinated approach: Collaborations have been launched with other high-quality Italian companies across other industrial sectors to promote a global idea of an Italian way, based on the shared values of respect for tradition and openness to innovation. Connections have been forged with the art world, the vital terrain of creativity.

The relationship with Piero Antinori is focused on a product, generating a new approach to leather dyeing. Meanwhile, other collaborations tie in with the Moreschi style more generally and focus on the value of the brand as a symbol of the Italian way. The link with Lurisia mineral water has resulted in a limited edition "Bolle Stille Winner Moreschi Limited Edition" exclusive bottle designed by Sottsass Associates for the finest Lurisia water and customized by Moreschi. This dual branded water was served during fashion week 2013 on the tables of the best Milanese restaurants such as Acanto, Al Pont de Ferr, Alice, Bacaro del Sambuco, Chic'n Quick Trattoria Moderna, Cucina del Toro, D'O, Il Baretto, Il Luogo di Aimo e Nadia, Il Salumaio, La Brisa, Osteria del Binari, Paper Moon, Pisacco, and Sadler.

Celebrating other distinctive characteristics of Moreschi shoes—lightness and agility—is the "Tender Mambo Bike Limited Edition" foldable bike, branded with the Moreschi logo and designed by famous Milanese designer AG Fronzoni in 1963. An environmentally friendly means of urban transport, it fits into a white leather bag with black detailing and can be transported as a trolley bag. In a panorama of movement, walking and cycling combine through a shared design based on lightness, quality, and innovation. Tender Mambo Bike has a double-thick aluminum frame in brilliant white, customized with the Moreschi logo designed by AG Fronzoni. It has a white bell with leather details and mambo stitching, BioLogic ergo handlebars, a BioLogic seat, Rotolo tires for the perfect glide, and ultra-compact, seven-speed gears. When folded its dimensions are 28 x 80 x 66 centimeters. It takes about fifteen seconds to fold it and place it in its bag. It weighs just eleven kilograms.

Limited-edition Tender Mambo Bike,
the Moreschi foldable bike.

Collaborations in the artistic field reveal the desire of Moreschi to open up to the Asian world through the perspective of unconventional artists like Li Chen, a Taoist Buddhist from Taiwan who was born in 1963. He expresses his philosophy in stylized human figures, hybrids of plump children, and mysterious divinities, which have made him famous in Asia and earned him his position of fifty-nine in the rankings of world artists put together by Artprice. Thanks to Moreschi, Li Chen exhibited for the first time in Milan during the Salone del Mobile in 2013.

In 2014, again during the Salone del Mobile, Moreschi presented the colored resin sculptures of Japanese artist Hiro Ando in its boutique in Piazza San Babila, sculptures inspired by the popular culture of his country. Cats, good luck symbols in Japan, are represented as samurais or sumo wrestlers and formed out of brightly colored resin. The clean, rounded forms recall the world of manga, interpreted through a neo-pop perspective.

Moreschi, a wise custodian of artisan tradition, has opened itself up to the global marketplace without abandoning its roots, in order to find new ideas from diverse sectors while maintaining and spreading its local qualities. Through this approach Moreschi has established itself as an ambassador of the "glocalism" that, according to the most perceptive sociologists, constitutes the fuel for a new modernity.

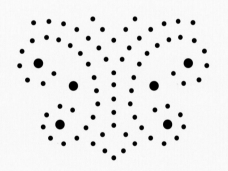

THE STORY
CONTINUES

" ALL TRULY
GREAT THOUGHTS
ARE CONCEIVED
WHILE WALKING. "

Friedrich Nietzsche

From Vigevano, Moreschi has set out to conquer the international market through franchising and investment in its own stores. There are over seven hundred commercial outlets in over eighty countries selling Moreschi products. The sundial housed in the Vigevano showroom is a reminder that at each time of the day, in some part of the world, there are people buying Moreschi shoes. In 1970, the first store was opened in Via Manzoni in Milan, specializing in men's shoes and run by Professor Mario Bonzanini. The following year, the boutique on Corso Vittorio Emanuele was added in what had been an old Perugina building. Its arrival was fought by the street's traders, who sent a petition to Milan City Hall signed by everyone except Bruno Magli, demanding that the concession of a shop license for a shoe brand be refused, as the area was already crowded with shoe shops. Nevertheless, the license was granted and soon after, in place of chocolates, it was shoes that were being sold. The opening of the flagship store in Milan, and the subsequent necessity to complete the product range, prompted Moreschi to complement the shoe collection with a line of accessories. The evolution has continued in the recent period with the inclusion of a women's collection of shoes and accessories that enriches the product offerings and contributes to highlighting and further strengthening the image and style of the brand.

The spacious shop in Milan is situated in Piazza San Babila, opposite the fountain, in the heart of the city center, a key hub for international clientele. It is spread across three floors and furnished in a classic style, with light wooden paneling and leather armchairs that give clients an immediate sense of comfort and the feeling of being in an elegant living room, rather than a shop. It reveals itself to be the ideal backdrop for the brand's style.

The shoes are lined up neatly along the shelves and are interspersed with a selection of accessories. Special care, the same care governing production at Vigevano, has been employed in the choice of materials and the attention to detail. For example, the top floor has been rendered with large chestnut leather floor panels—a strategic choice that lends a particular warmth to the environment, reaffirming in an experiential way the vocation of the brand. Two high and wide window fronts provide an exhibition setting for the collections, offering even to hurried passers-by an overview and an immediate idea of the Moreschi style.

The interior design, the choice of materials, the furnishings, and the careful positioning of the products render the Milan flagship store not just an enticing place, but an effective gallery of the collections and DNA of the brand.

〰〰〰〰〰

Opposite: The Moreschi boutique in Piazza San Babila
Previous pages: The Moreschi store on
Via Frattina, Rome.

229

In small catalogs from the 1960s, the models of men's shoes in production are illustrated. The multiplicity of models are the pride of the company, which distinguishes itself from its competitors by the large variety of its styles.

Mario leafs through them, appreciating their diversity and remarking on their modernity, pausing on the elegant, tapered cut that, updated in proportion, has always distinguished Moreschi shoes. "Our most successful forms," he says, "have always been pointed, elongated, or semi-squared. The ideal Moreschi proportions are two-fifths for the back and three-fifths for the front. The ratio has not changed in thirty years even if, reflecting foot sizes, the shoes have steadily grown a centimeter in width and two in length."

"To celebrate our anniversary," he concludes, "we decided to present a capsule of shoes, made by reworking AG Fronzoni's albums of trends."

Once again, as throughout the company's history, the future roots itself in the past to anchor alongside innovation the sure value of a tradition cultivated with passion and skill.

〰〰〰

Opposite:
The globe in GianBeppe's office.
Moreschi distributes in more than eighty countries
around the world.

"

I FEEL LIKE A CHILD
OF LEATHER AND SKIN.
I STILL FEEL EXCITEMENT
WHENEVER I ENTER
THE 'SAFE' WHERE
WE AGE THE LEATHER.

"

Mario Moreschi

"
THE TRUE TREASURE
OF THIS COMPANY
IS THE DESIRE TO IMPROVE
TOGETHER DAY AFTER DAY
LIKE A BIG FAMILY.
„

Stefano Moreschi

"

WE HAVE A GREAT
STORY TO TELL,
BUT WHAT REALLY COUNTS
IS THE UNIQUE EXPERIENCE
AND FEELING OF WEARING
OUR SHOES. "

Francesco Moreschi

PHOTOGRAPHY CREDITS

RARO CADE CHI BEN CAMMINA

Leonardo da Vinci

"He who walks straight rarely falls."
LEONARDO DA VINCI

Printed in October 2015
by EBS - Verona, Italy